WORLD-CLASS BRAIDING
Manes & Tails

A Tack Trunk Reference Guide

CAT HILL AND EMMA FORD

WITH PHOTOGRAPHS BY JESSICA DAILEY

TRAFALGAR SQUARE
North Pomfret, Vermont

First published in 2021 by
Trafalgar Square Books
North Pomfret, Vermont 05053

Disclaimer of Liability
The authors and publisher shall have neither liability nor responsibility to any person or entity with respect to any loss or damage caused or alleged to be caused directly or indirectly by the information contained in this book. While the book is as accurate as the authors can make it, there may be errors, omissions, and inaccuracies.

Trafalgar Square Books encourages the use of approved safety helmets in all equestrian sports and activities.

Library of Congress Cataloging-in-Publication Data
Names: Hill, Catherine, 1981- author. | Ford, Emma, 1976- author. | Daily, Jessica, photographer.
Title: World-class braiding manes and tails : a tack trunk reference guide / Cat Hill and Emma Ford ; with photographs by Jessica Dailey.
Description: North Pomfret, Vermont : Trafalgar Square Books, 2021. | Summary: "Professional grooms Cat Hill and Emma Ford, co-authors of the bestselling World-Class Grooming for Horses, have braided thousands of horses for a variety of disciplines over the course of their esteemed careers in the equestrian industry. Now they've highlighted those skills in a book conceived to be a helpful barn companion-one you can take with you and keep in your tack trunk, providing a go-to reference whenever you need it. Chock full of full-color photographs that illustrate every step of the process"-- Provided by publisher.
Identifiers: LCCN 2020045471 | ISBN 9781646010578 (spiral bound)
Subjects: LCSH: Horses--Grooming. | Braid.
Classification: LCC SF285.7 .H545 2021 | DDC 636.1/083--dc23
LC record available at https://lccn.loc.gov/2020045471

All photographs by Jessica Dailey except page 15, top
Book design by Elizabeth Gray
Cover design by RM Didier
Typefaces: Open Sans, Poppl-Pontifex BE, Helvetica

Printed in China
10 9 8 7 6 5 4 3 2 1

Contents

Introduction

Braids can make or break the hard work of turning a horse out nicely. The only way to get really good at braiding your own horse is to practice in low-pressure moments, at home, when you have time and can reject the ones you don't like and admire the ones you do. We've crafted this reference so you can keep it in your tack trunk, and whenever you are at the barn with a few extra minutes, you can put a couple braids in! Our advice is to put a few braids in at least a couple times a week until you get the hang of it. In our experience, when you just put one or two braids in, but you do it often, you actually increase your skill more than the occasional, hour-long, full braiding session.

Included in these pages are the basics of good braids—the fundamentals, if you will. Once you master braiding down, switching from hunter braids to event braids to dressage braids is easy. We have also included a few new styles for more traditional-looking braids on horses with long manes. As we have traveled and groomed for others, we have found that many people don't like to pull or shorten their horses' manes. The new braiding techniques we have added address this. They are also a great way for children to learn how to

Facing page, from left to right: Photographer Jessica Dailey, co-author Cat Hill with her daughter Adelaide, and co-author Emma Ford with Mystery Whisper and her dog Charlie.

braid properly because leaving the mane longer makes it easier for small hands to handle.

One last thing: Horses show affection to each other by grooming each other, often on the neck. Braiding a little bit, and doing it often, can increase your bond with your horse, and convince him that it is a fun activity, rather than a tortuous event. That's a win, even if you aren't competing!

Braiding the Mane

• *Button braids* are the neat, round knots that are seen on eventers, show jumpers, and dressage horses. They are accomplished the same way in all three disciplines, with the only difference being the amount of hair gathered in the original braid. How much hair you gather will determine the size of the "button" at the end of the job.

• *Hunter* or *flat braids* are worn exclusively by show hunters. These braids should lie flat on the neck with a very small, raised knob at the top of the braid.

• A *running braid* is a single continuous braid that runs down the length of the horse's neck. It is used on horses that are kept with a full, long mane.

• Many horses wear longer manes or don't like having their manes pulled, so we've provided additional braiding options for these scenarios.

✦ Gather Your Tools

1 You will need the following:

• Yarn or crochet thread (for sewing braids). When preparing your yarn or thread for braiding, grasp the end of the yarn in the fold of your thumb and pointer finger, then wrap around your elbow and back up, repeat this until you have the desired number of pieces. Cut the loops you have created near your hand. This should result in yarn strands 25 to 30 inches long.
• Rubber bands (if braiding with bands).
• Wax or Exhibitor's™ Quic Braid™ spray (to help secure the braids).
• A fine-tooth comb.

• Small, sharp scissors.
• A pull-through (available through most tack shops or at a craft store as a "rug hook").
• A large-eye blunt yarn needle.
• A "crocodile" hair clip (to hold hair out of the way).
• A stool.

✦ Braiding Down

Braiding down is the process of braiding a tight, even braid down from the crest and securing it. It is the most important step in any braiding process. Without a nice, tight, smooth braid, no final design will look good. First, we discuss how to braid down, then show you how to finish off with rubber bands, yarn, or thread, plus tell you the correct way to remove the braids.

Note: We are using white-colored thread, yarn, and rubber bands to help demonstrate the steps. When in competition, use a color that matches your horse's mane. We are using two different-colored manes for demonstration here.

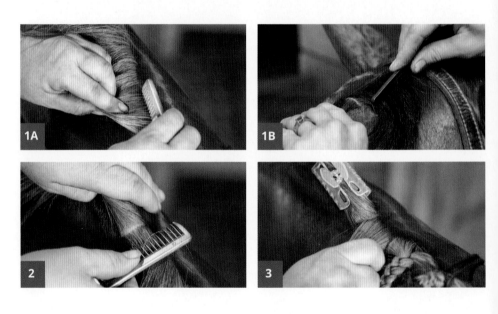

1 A & B Separate the mane to be braided. The amount of hair will depend on what type of style you are creating: *button braids* can be small-, medium-, or large-diameter. *Dressage* horses use large-diameter braids, so separate 5 to 6 inches of hair (about the width of your palm). *Show jumpers* wear medium-diameter braids, so separate 3 to 5 inches of hair (about four fingers). *Eventers* go in small-diameter braids, so separate 2 to 3 inches of hair (about two or three fingers). *Show hunters* should have very narrow braids, so no more than 2 inches of hair should be separated.

2 Make sure the part is straight.

3 Sections can be secured either by using rubber bands or a crocodile clip.

Braiding Down (Cont.)

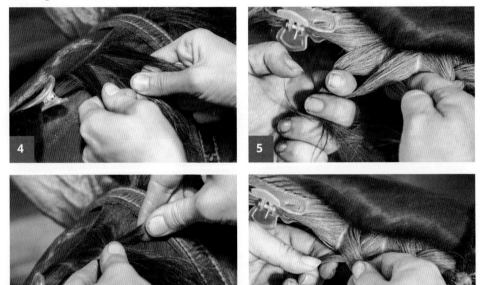

4 Separate the section into three equal portions.

5 Cross the right strand over the center strand, using your thumb to keep it lying flat and down.

6 A & B Next cross the left side over the right, pulling the center piece to the right. Again, use your thumbs to hold in place and smooth.

pro tip

For those manes that always have flyaway hairs, use some form of mousse—Shapley's™ Mane Mousse™ or a beeswax—to smooth the hairs into the braid as you begin braiding down.

Continued ▶

Braiding Down (Cont.)

7 A & B Continue crossing right to left and left to right down the braid. Make sure to pull across, not down.

Now the technique continues, but varies according to the equipment used: rubber bands, thread, or yarn.

✦ Using Rubber Bands

1 A & B When using rubber bands, braid as far down as you can.

2 Wrap the rubber band several times around the braid, leaving yourself a large amount of rubber band held in a large loop.

Using Rubber Bands (Cont.)

3 Fold the braid up, using your middle finger to hold the rubber band and your pointer finger to create a smooth fold.

4 Holding the braid steady, loop the rubber band around the folded braid.

5 Continue holding the rubber band out; you will now have a folded end and a "tail" of hair lying parallel to your braid.

6 Repeatedly loop the rubber band up the braid until all the loose ends are tucked away.

✦ Using Thread or Yarn

1 When you get two-thirds of the way down the braid, or are 2 to 3 inches from the end, take a piece of your thread (or yarn), fold it in half, and incorporate half of it with the piece of hair about to be braided.

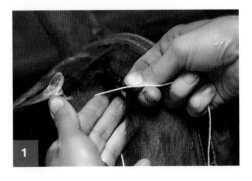

Continued ▶

pro tip

When working with a weak, thin mane, don't start the braid too tight at the crest. This will help prevent hair being pulled out. The first four crossovers should *not* create a pull on the crest, but from then on, the braid should be tight. Avoid using rubber bands on weak manes; this will only pull out more hair.

Using Thread or Yarn (Cont.)

2 Braid the next piece of hair over, and incorporate the other half of the thread, as shown.

3 Continue braiding with the thread as if it is another strand of hair for four or five crosses. Then, separate the hair into one hand and thread into the other.

4 Loop the yarn around the braid and through the loop.

5 Pull snugly to tighten the knot.

6 All finished.

✦ Finishing Braids with Rubber Bands

This form of braiding is a great way to learn and for more experienced braiders, it's a quick and efficient method. Follow the steps for "Using Rubber Bands" to braid using a rubber band.

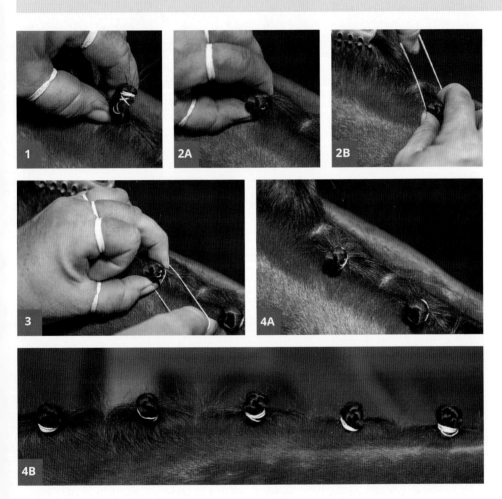

1 Fold the tip under toward the crest of the neck.

2 A & B Fold in half again and place a rubber band around the entire button.

3 For extra security, place a second rubber band around the button.

4 A & B They can look quite professional when done correctly.

✦ Removing Rubber Bands

Leaving a mane braided with rubber bands overnight is not ideal: some horses find the bands "pull" too much on their crest and try to rub them out.

1 Put your thumb and forefinger on the top and bottom of the braid.

2 Pull the braid toward you and it will unfold.

3 Remove the bands.

✦ Finishing Simple Sewn-In Button Braids

This form of braiding is the classic hunt braid, and for good reason. It is very customizable and will stay tight no matter what the weather or activity. Use cotton crochet thread or waxed-cotton braiding thread in the braid. Nylon crochet thread is hard to knot.

1 Thread both hanging ends through the eye of a large-eye, blunt yarn needle.

Finishing Simple Sewn-In Button Braids (Cont.)

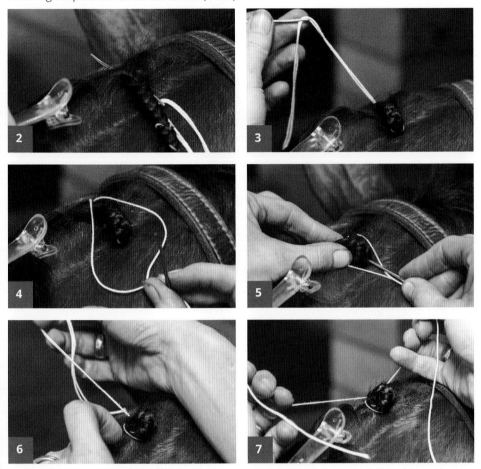

2 Push the needle through the center of the braid.

3 Pull up on the string until the braid folds in half.

4 Holding the needle in your hand, split the thread and put one strand on either side of the braid.

5 Roll the braid up and push your needle through the lowest point of the "roll."

6 Pull up on the thread until quite tight, removing the needle.

7 Split the strands again, and wrap the outside of the braid.

Continued ▶

Finishing Simple Sewn-In Button Braids (Cont.)

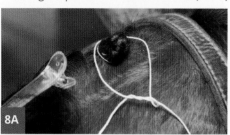

pro tip

When doing button braids, the thicker the mane, the narrower the selection of hair you should take for each braid. This will be easier to fold up in order to create the button braid. If you want large button braids for a dressage horse, know that a longer-length mane makes a thick button easier to fold up.

8 A & B Cross the thread twice then pull tight.

9 Cross the thread once more to secure the knot.

10 Cut the ends close to the neck.

11 Finished sewn-in button braids.

✦ Removing Sewn-In Button Braids

1 A & B To remove, simply cut the knot at the bottom of the button. Pull the braid down...

2 A & B ...and cut the knot at the end of the braid.

3 When a horse's braids have been removed, the mane will look as if it's had a bad perm! It is not a good idea to leave a horse's mane like this for any length of time. Do not assume the mane will just flatten on its own; if the braids were sewn in, it can take several days for the mane to "un-crimp." Prior to undoing your braids, simply take a damp sponge and wet the mane. This will make removing the braids faster and will help to smooth the mane down. Once the braids are pulled out, run the sponge over it again and use a fine-toothed comb to smooth it out.

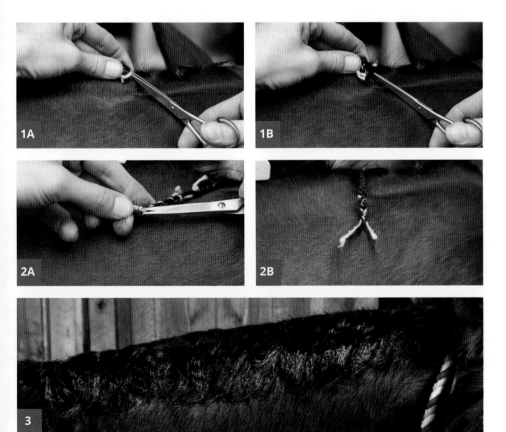

✦ Yarn Button Braids—The Emma Ford Way

Very similar to sewn-in braids, this braiding method stays in very well and works on a variety of manes.

1 Place your forefinger and middle finger of your right hand on the underside, close to the crest.

2 Using your left hand, twist the braid to the right and over the top of the crest.

3 Using your fingers to maintain the loop, grab the yarn.

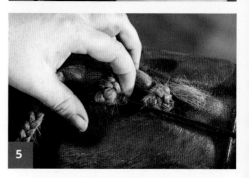

4 Push the yarn into the loop you have created then pull the entire braid through the loop to the right.

5 To keep it tight, use your left hand at the base to help feed it through the loop.

Yarn Button Braids (Cont.)

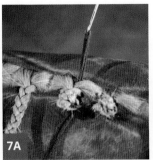

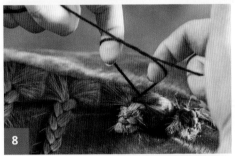

6 Insert a pull-through down through the center of the braid, close to the crest.

7 A & B Pull the loose yarn back through the braid.

8 Separate the two pieces of yarn, wrap one piece to the left and the other to the right. Maintaining the loop, cross the yarn ends twice.

9 Pull the loop tight at the bottom of the braid.

10 Cut off loose yarn close to the knot.

11 Emma Ford button braids.

✦ Removing Yarn Button Braids

To remove these braids, use a seam ripper. Note: You'll need good lighting to make sure you don't rip out the hair by mistake.

1 Look under the braid and there should be a "cross" of yarn.

2 Cut the cross carefully.

3 Unknot the braid.

4 Use the seam ripper carefully at the end of the braid in a downward motion to release the original knot that holds the long braid in place.

5 Pull out the yarn and undo the braid.

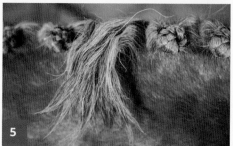

✦ Hunter Braids

This type of braiding is primarily seen in the hunter ring—anywhere from 30 to 50 even braids down the entire neck. This takes time to learn; however, when done well, it looks beautiful. The key to proper hunter braids is a very evenly pulled mane. Use a comb with tight teeth when combing out the hair; this helps to smooth down any errant hairs.

1 When braiding down, the braids should sit no more than half an inch away from each other. You want the braids to almost touch when done, so start with a braid no wider than your index finger.

2 Using a pull-through, put it down the very center of the braid at the crest.

3 Hook both ends of yarn with your pull-through.

pro tip

Are you new to braiding? Although having a squeaky clean mane for top turnout is ideal, braiding such a mane, especially when you're new to braiding, will be harder, as the mane will be quite slippery. Plan on washing your horse's mane two to three days prior to a show.

Continued ▶

Hunter Braids (Cont.)

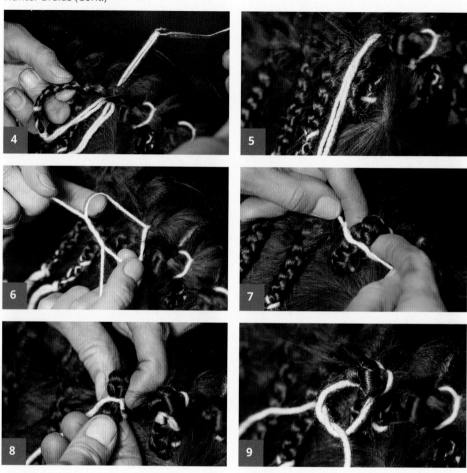

4 Pull the loose strings through the top of the crest.

5 Pull the end of the braid into the bottom of the crest but not all the way through. It should make a flat fold that lies on the neck.

6 Separate the pieces of string. Make a loop by crossing the ends over themselves twice.

7 Using your fingers to hold the braid up slightly, tighten the knot down. This will create a small knob.

8 If necessary, straighten the sides so the knob lies perpendicular to the crest.

9 Finish the knot with another cross-over.

pro tip

When deciding how far down the neck to go with your braids, set your saddle pad in the correct position. Mark with a rubber band or clip where the saddle pad hits, then braid to that spot. Some horses can be fussy about braids on their withers, so be gentle and braid a slight bit looser than you do the rest of the mane. Hunter horses that will be jogged and event horses braided for the formal jog should have all of the mane hair braided.

Hunter Braids (Cont.)

10 Cut the thread close to the braid.

11 In this photo, we've demonstrated a couple of common mistakes, plus included a correct braid for comparison, from right to left.

Wrong: Braid One has a decent knob, but the loop has slid apart. This is generally caused by braiding down with uneven sections of hair.

Wrong: Braid Two has a knob that is a bit too large, and it sits too far off the neck. You can catch this before the knot is finished and bring a little less hair into the braid.

Braid Three is just right.

12 Finished hunter braids.

✦ Running Braid

Essentially one single French braid, you generally see this form of braiding on dressage horses with long manes, especially Baroque breeds such as Friesians and Andalusians. The mane is braided on whichever side of the neck the mane lies naturally.

1 A & B Start at the poll and divide the mane into three sections. Cross the right over the center.

2 Cross the left over the right.

3 Next, start the "running" part of the braid. Cross the right over the center again, then the left over the right.

4 Section off a small part of the mane and add it to the section you just crossed over the center.

5 Cross the right over the center, holding it as close as possible to the crest. Do not add any more hair from the right.

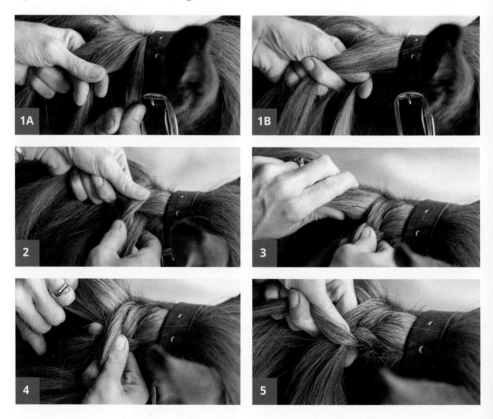

Running Braid (Cont.)

6 Using your right hand to support the braid, add new hair with your left hand, crossing the left over the center again.

7 Again, bring the left over the center without adding any hair. Pull tightly and smooth with your thumbs to keep the braid close to the crest.

if you pull tightly enough, the braid will start to "roll" so you can see the underside of it instead of the side.

8 A–D Continue this way down the neck, making sure you stay close to the crest.

Continued ▶

Running Braid (Cont.)

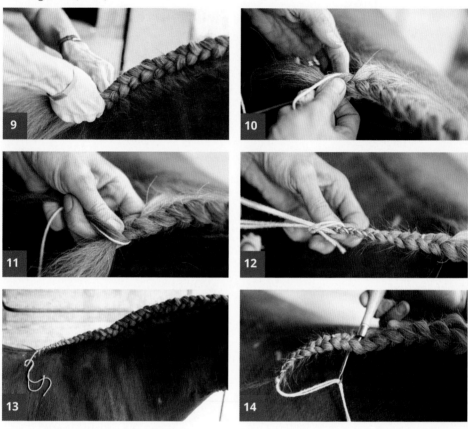

9 As you approach the withers, the braid should sit close to the crest, with the underside clearly visible.

10 When you reach the end of the mane, add a piece of yarn or thread 25 to 30 inches long, laying it behind the braid and then grasping each end of the strand in its own section of hair.

11 Incorporate each end of the yarn into the braid.

12 When you are almost out of hair, loop both ends of the yarn around the end of the braid and pull the ends through the loop to tie it off.

13 Your braid should look like this. You can trim the yarn and leave it like this, or tie up the end of the braid for a more finished look.

14 To tie up the end of your running braid, push a pull-through (or rug hook) into the center of the braid where the "running" part finishes.

Running Braid (Cont.)

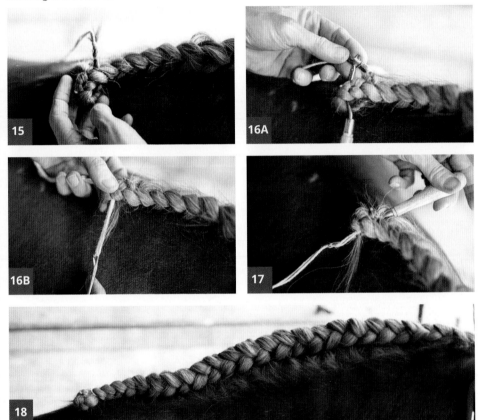

15 Pull the end up through the center of the braid.

16 A & B Next, from below the braid, insert your pull-through into the loop of braid you've created. Hook the tail of the braid and the yarn above, then pull the tail and yarn back down through the loop of braid.

17 Now move down the braid and insert your pull-through from top down, hooking just the yarn ends

and pulling them back up through the running braid.

18 Move the pull-through toward the ears by one braid section, and push the pull-through up through the braid instead of down. Pull just one end of the yarn down through the braid, so you have one piece of yarn above the braid and one below the braid. Tie the two yarn pieces together at the top of the braid, creating a tidy finished product.

✦ Braiding Unpulled Manes

This method of braiding works well for horses competing in dressage or eventing that have unpulled manes. It is a very simple way to braid and is excellent for children, beginner braiders, and professionals alike because it produces really lovely results without a complicated process. It is a nice alternative to a running braid since the braids can be left in longer, and don't stretch out or rumple as easily.

1 Begin with a clean, well-combed mane. Do not use a silicone spray on the mane or the braids won't hold. If the mane is very tangle-prone, use a conditioner when you wash it. Starting right behind the halter, divide out a section of hair about 3 to 4 inches wide.

2 Begin braiding down (see p. 2), tightly pulling right over left.

pro tip

If your horse doesn't like having his mane pulled, do any tidying up at least a week before you need to braid. It also helps to pull a little hair often, rather than pulling the entire mane all at once. A big pull can create a lot of discomfort for a sensitive horse. Pulling a mane the same day you need to braid will only cause your horse to be anxious while braiding.

Braiding Unpulled Manes (Cont.)

3 A–C Only braid for three to five crossovers; then grasp the braid tightly with one hand and put a rubber band around it. (It is important for the braid to stay snug.) The first braid should look like a very short braid with a nice long tail.

4 Now comes the fun part! You can use a Topsy Tail Plait Puller or simply a piece of wire folded into a loop with the top twisted together. Push the loop down through the center of the base of the braid.

5 When the loop is pushed all the way through the mane, pull the tail of the braid through the loop, as if you are threading a needle.

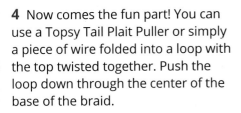

Continued ▶

Braiding Unpulled Manes (Cont.)

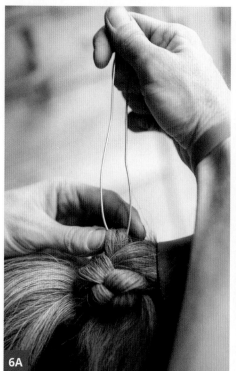

6 A & B Using the loop, pull the tail of the braid up through the base of the braid. This will create a small folded braid. Pull the tail all the way out at the top.

7 Now, leave that braid and divide the next section of mane, 3 to 4 inches wide.

8 A & B Grasp the tail of the first braid, and add it to the new section of mane.

Braiding Unpulled Manes (Cont.)

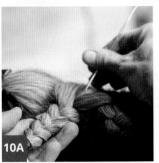

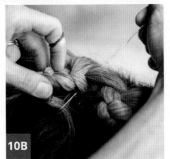

9 A & B Braid three to five crossovers, including the tail of the old braid as part of the new section of hair, then secure this second braid with a rubber band at the end.

10 A–C Insert the wire loop through the center of the base of the second braid, thread the tail of the braid through the loop, and pull it through the braid base.

11 A & B Repeat these steps down the horse's neck. Each braid will have a small "bridge" from it to the next.

Continued ▶

Braiding Unpulled Manes (Cont.)

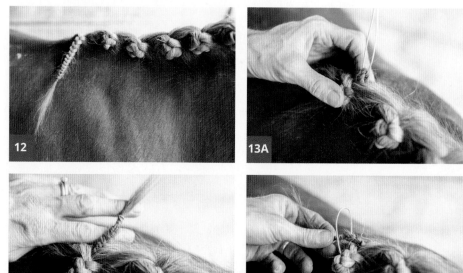

12 When you reach the end of the mane, braid the last braid down farther than the previous braids, about 6 to 7 inches, then secure it with a rubber band.

13 A & B Using your loop, pull the braid through the middle of its base

so the braided tail sticks up.

14 A–C Now, push your loop through the folded braid, right to left, and pull the remaining tail completely through the wire loop and then through the folded braid.

Braiding Unpulled Manes (Cont.)

15 A & B Grasp the wispy tail of the braid with your left hand and pull it toward the withers, then wrap a rubber band around the whole rolled braid.

16 The finished product: an elegant neck.

For a slightly fancier version of this braid for unpulled manes, you can braid the hair "bridge" between braids. This requires a more advanced level of skill because the braiding must be very tight and must be secured well for it to look sharp.

1 Begin the same as for the simple version (p. 22), but braid very far down the braid, close to the end of the hair. You will need at least 6 to 7 inches of braid.

Continued ▶

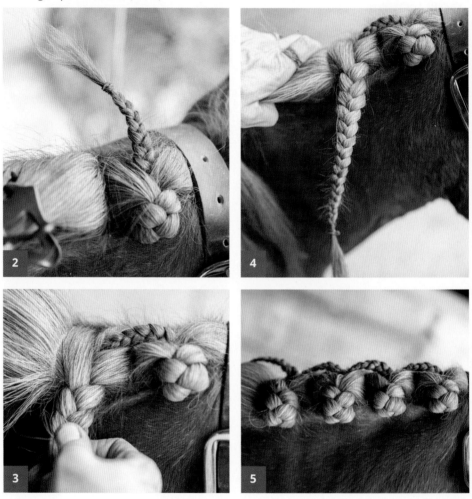

2 As with the previous method, use a wire loop to pull the braid all the way through its base.

3 Divide out your next section of hair, incorporating the tail of the previous braid into the new braid.

4 Braid the new braid down until you are again near the end of the hair.

5 Repeat this pattern as you progress down the horse's neck, creating a beautiful bridge between each braid.

Braiding the Forelock

The finishing touch to your braided mane is a tidy forelock. There are two methods for braiding a forelock: a simple braid with a button and a French braid tucked away. The simple braid can easily be accomplished with a rubber band and looks nice as long as the horse's mane is not too thick or long. It should be noted that a rubber band braid is *not* appropriate for hunters. A French braid gives a really professional finish but is hard to accomplish on a thin or short forelock.

✦ Simple Forelock Braid

*The simple braid can easily be accomplished with a rubber band and looks nice as long as the horse's mane is not too thick or long. It should be noted that a rubber band braid like this is **not** appropriate for hunters.*

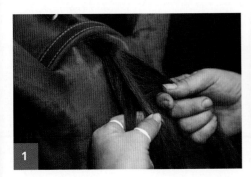

1 Comb the forelock and separate into three equal sections. Have rubber bands on your fingers.

2 Cross the right side over the center section.

Continued ▶

pro tip

Stress can make braiding harder. Do a timed run-through the week before a show or performance so you know how much time you need to finish braiding your horse.

Simple Forelock Braid (Cont.)

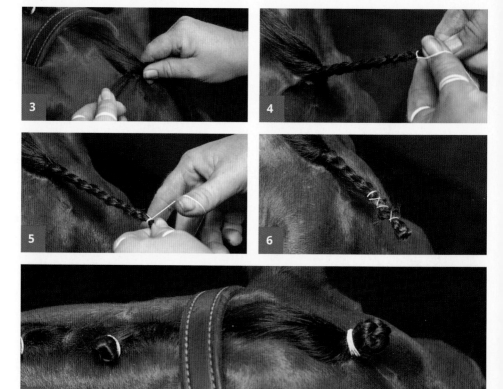

3 Then take the left over the center, making sure to pull nice and tight.

4 Continue braiding until you get close to the end.

5 Secure the end of the braid.

6 Fold up the loose hair and use rubber bands to attach it to the braid.

7 Roll up the braid and secure with a rubber band.

✦ French Braid

A French braid gives a really professional finish but is hard to accomplish on a thin or short forelock.

1 Comb out the forelock carefully. Use your large-eye, blunt-end yarn needle to separate out a section of hair from the top of the forelock.

2 Divide this section into two even pieces.

3 Cross the right piece over the left.

4 Add a section of hair of equal thickness to the two you are already holding from the outside of the *right* side of the forelock. Cross this over to use as your third strand of braid.

5 Separate out a narrow section of hair from the outside of the *left* side of the forelock.

Continued ▶

French Braid (Cont.)

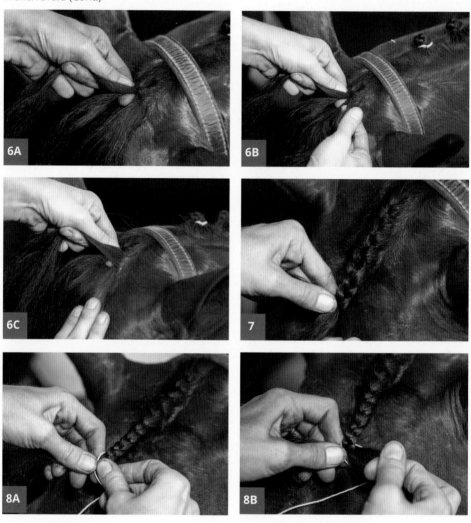

6 A–C Each time you cross over, French braid by adding a narrow section of hair from only the outside.

7 Continue adding only from the outside, until you reach the bottom of the braid, then gather up the remaining hair into the braid.

8 A & B Braid a half-inch below the end of the French braid and add your thread by crossing it behind the hair.

French Braid (Cont.)

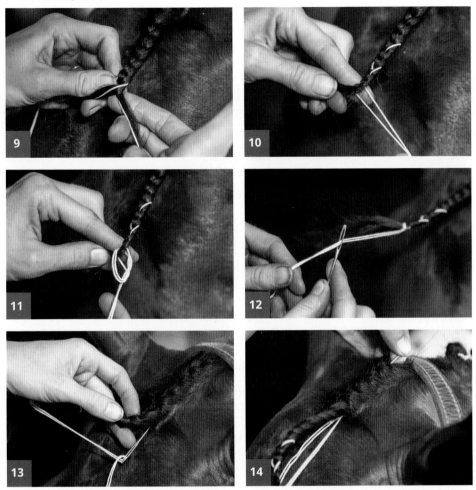

9 Incorporate the two strands of thread into the braid.

10 Continue braiding until you have about one inch of hair left. Separate the threads into one hand and the braid into the other, holding the braid tight.

11 Tie off the end of the braid with a simple knot.

12 Thread both ends through your large-eye, blunt-end yarn needle.

13 Being careful not to stab your horse in the head, thread the needle into the center of the French braid.

14 You want it to emerge in the very top of the braid, dead center.

Continued ▶

French Braid (Cont.)

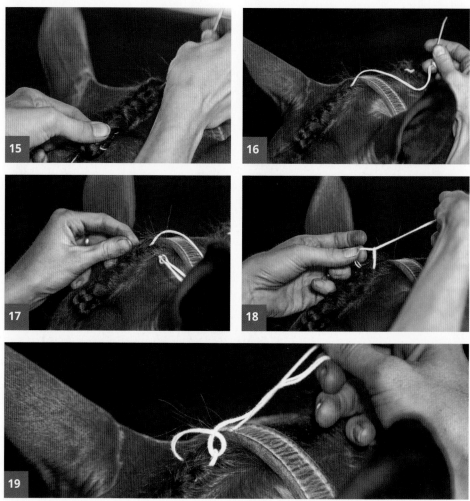

15 Pull the braid up into the hollow area you've created by only pulling from the sides of the forelock in the French braid. You may need to use your finger to help guide it.

16 It should fold in half and lie smoothly next to the forehead.

17 Run your needle underneath the braid.

18 Use the needle to thread through the loop you made on the right.

19 Next thread through the loop on the left.

French Braid (Cont.)

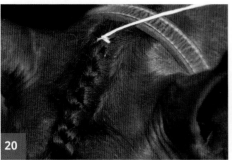

20

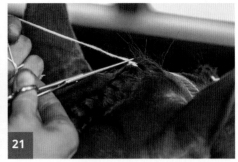

21

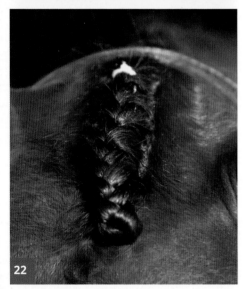

22

pro tip

Practice making a few braids every day, rather than confining yourself to big, long braiding sessions. The repetition of doing it regularly will improve your ability sooner and with less stress.

20 Pull nice and tight.

21 Cut the thread close to the forelock.

22 You will end with a very tidy, tight French braid with no evidence of its end.

Braiding the Tail

Braiding a tail is time-consuming and must be practiced, so make sure you hone your skill at home before heading to the ring. We use a combination of a French braid and a regular braid to create the look.

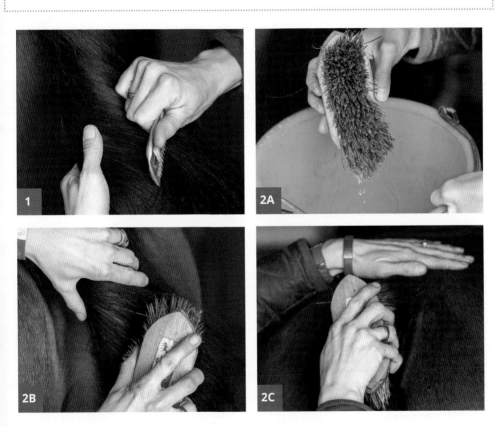

1 Start by combing the tail down very well, especially the sides and back of the dock. There should be no conditioner at the top of the tail.

2 A–C Dampen a brush with a bit of water. Then brush the sides and back of the dock so the hair is damp.

Continued ▶

Tail Braiding (Cont.)

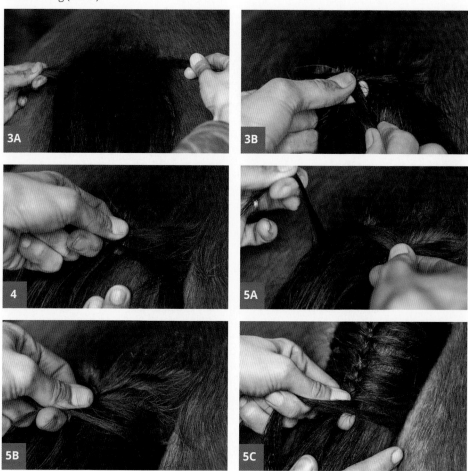

3 A & B Separate out a small section of hair from the top corner of each side of the tail, bring to the middle, and cross right over left.

4 Separate out another small section of hair from the left side of the tail and cross over the two strands in the middle. These pieces will be your three strands to braid.

5 A & B Alternating sides, bring a very small section of hair from the outermost area of the dock into the middle and incorporate into the strand you are working with.

5 C This will create a French braid with very narrow strips of hair coming from the outside of the tail into the center of the braid.

Tail Braiding (Cont.)

6 A & B When you get to the bottom of the dock, drop a small amount of hair from each of the three sections. Do this by splitting the section as you cross it over the center.

7 Continue with a regular braid for about 6 more inches; add in your yarn.

8 A & B Braid one or two more times, then tie the braid. First, cross one strand of yarn over the top of the braid...

9 ...then the other way.

10 Cross your yarn over itself twice to create a surgical knot.

Continued ▶

Tail Braiding (Cont.)

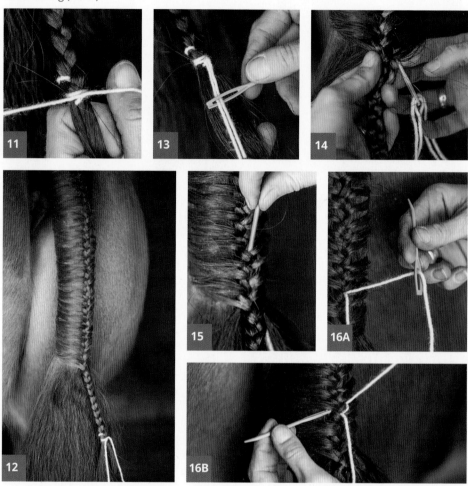

11 Tighten it down securely.

12 The braid should be tight and even.

13 Now thread the yarn through a large-eye, blunt-end yarn needle.

14 Push the needle behind the braid.

15 Come out the center of the braid about 3 inches up the braid.

16 A & B Keep one piece of yarn in the needle and go straight behind the braid, coming out the other side.

Tail Braiding (Cont.)

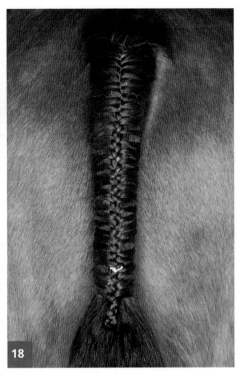

17 A & B Tie a secure knot and trim the ends.

18 A nice, tidy tail braid.

pro tip

During the winter in the north, our horses have several months off competition. I like to bang their tails quite short after their last fall competition. I do this for two reasons: First, it keeps the tail out of icy mud that can damage and break it. Second, the tail gets a chance to grow in more thickly for the next season since I trim to above any split ends that cause a thin, wispy-looking bottom. I find my charges' tails stay much thicker when I do this. —*Cat*

ALSO AVAILABLE

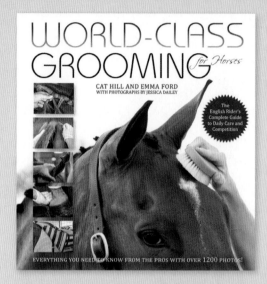

"It's all there in one spiral-bound book, making it a great resource for experienced horsemen and novices alike, and it should be considered required reading for those looking into working student or groom positions. ... Whether you're looking for instructions on how to do hunter braids, wrap a leg properly, or adjust a figure-eight noseband, you can be sure Ford and Hill have done it thousands of times, and they're eager to share their knowledge."

CHRONICLE OF THE HORSE

"Top grooms Cat Hill and Emma Ford demonstrate how to clean the horse from nose to tail; wrap, clip, braid, and ship him; prepare him for competition; and care for him after work or showing so he is rested and ready to do it all again."

NEW YORK HORSE

Contact professional grooms Cat Hill and Emma Ford about their educational clinics for all ages:

WorldClassGrooming.com
Facebook: @worldclassgroomingforhorses
Instagram: @worldclassgrooming